# BRINGING BACK THE

# Gray Wolf

## Cynthia O'Brien

CRABTREE
PUBLISHING COMPANY
WWW.CRABTREEBOOKS.COM

# CRABTREE
## PUBLISHING COMPANY
### WWW.CRABTREEBOOKS.COM

**Author:** Cynthia O'Brien

**Series Research and Development:** Reagan Miller

**Managing Editor:** Tim Cooke

**Picture Manager:** Sophie Mortimer

**Design Manager:** Keith Davis

**Editorial Director:** Lindsey Lowe

**Children's Publisher:** Anne O'Daly

**Editor:** Ellen Rodger

**Proofreader:** Lorna Notsch

**Cover design:** Margaret Amy Salter

**Production coordinator and**
 **Prepress technician:** Margaret Amy Salter

**Print coordinator:** Katherine Berti

Produced for Crabtree Publishing Company
by Brown Bear Books

Photographs (t=top, b= bottom, l=left, r=right, c=center)

**Front Cover:** All images from Shutterstock

**Interior:** Alamy: Design Pics inc, 24, National Geographic Creative, 19t, WheskeyWolf, 6; Defenders of Wildlife: Wood River Wolf Project, 18; Getty Images: Bettmann, 9b, William Campbell, 8, 14-15, 21; iStock: Jan T Bost, 7, Ken Canning, 1, 13, Darius Cheng, 22-23, dss images, 5, S Eyerkaufer, 25, Fulltimedreamers, 19b, Steve Geer, 4, HakuNellies, 20, Judi Len, 29, lissart, 16-17, Mile High Traveler, 15, John Pitcher, 20, B G Smith, 23, A B Zerit, 26-27; National Parks Conservation Association: 11; Public Domain: Michael Runtz, 27b, US Federal Government, 17; Shutterstock: FH Even, 12, Stanley Ford, 27t, Franck Palaticky, 9t, Tom Reichner, 10.

Brown Bear Books has made every attempt to contact the copyright holder. If you have any information please contact licensing@ brownbearbooks.co.uk

**Library and Archives Canada Cataloguing in Publication**

O'Brien, Cynthia (Cynthia J.), author
 Bringing back the gray wolf / Cynthia O'Brien.

(Animals back from the brink)
Includes index.
Issued in print and electronic formats.
ISBN 978-0-7787-4903-5 (hardcover).--
ISBN 978-0-7787-4909-7 (softcover).--
ISBN 978-1-4271-2103-5 (HTML)

 1. Gray wolf--Juvenile literature. 2. Gray wolf--Conservation--Juvenile literature. 3. Endangered species--Juvenile literature. 4. Wildlife recovery--Juvenile literature. I. Title.

QL737.C22O27 2018          j333.95'977316          C2018-903049-6
                                                    C2018-903050-X

**Library of Congress Cataloging-in-Publication Data**

Names: O'Brien, Cynthia (Cynthia J.), author.
Title: Bringing back the gray wolf / Cynthia O'Brien.
Description: New York, New York : Crabtree Publishing, [2019] |
 Series: Animals back from the brink | Includes index.
Identifiers: LCCN 2018036859 (print) | LCCN 2018037480 (ebook) |
 ISBN 9781427121035 (Electronic) |
 ISBN 9780778749035 (hardcover : alk. paper) |
 ISBN 9780778749097 (paperback : alk. paper)
Subjects: LCSH: Gray wolf--United States--Conservation--Juvenile
 literature.
Classification: LCC QL737.C22 (ebook) |
 LCC QL737.C22 O27 2019 (print) | DDC 599.773--dc23
LC record available at https://lccn.loc.gov/2018036859

# Crabtree Publishing Company
www.crabtreebooks.com          1-800-387-7650

Printed in the U.S.A./102018/CG20180810

**Published in Canada**
**Crabtree Publishing**
616 Welland Ave.
St. Catharines, Ontario
L2M 5V6

**Published in the United States**
**Crabtree Publishing**
PMB 59051
350 Fifth Avenue, 59th Floor
New York, New York 10118

**Published in the United Kingdom**
**Crabtree Publishing**
Maritime House
Basin Road North, Hove
BN41 1WR

**Published in Australia**
**Crabtree Publishing**
3 Charles Street
Coburg North
VIC, 3058

# Contents

Find videos and extra material online at **crabtreeplus.com** to learn more about the conservation of animals and ecosystems. See page 30 in this book for the access code to this material.

# The Disappearing Gray Wolf

Wolves once lived across North America, Europe, and Asia. By the 1930s, however, gray wolves had almost disappeared from North America. People hunted them until there were few left. The wolf had been **exterminated** from **Atlantic Canada** by the early 1900s. It survived only in parts of northern Canada. In the United States, except Alaska, the situation was **critical** by the 1970s. A few hundred wolves lived in two small areas: northern Minnesota and Isle Royale in Michigan.

Gray wolves are the largest of the dog family. In spite of their name, these wolves can have brown, black, white, or reddish fur. Gray wolves live in mountains, and forests and on the **tundra**.

# THE GOOD AND THE BAD WOLF

Humans and wolves have lived together for centuries. People around the world included wolves in their myths. Some stories showed great respect for the wolf as a powerful hunter. Roman soldiers and Native American warriors wore wolf skins as a sign of strength, for example. Native Americans lived in harmony with the wolf for thousands of years. Many tribes still honor it in their dances and ceremonies. For them, the wolf is a strong, noble creature. They respect its hunting skills and its wisdom. But not everyone sees the wolf in the same way. Other stories reflected a dislike of wolves because they attacked **livestock** and even people. The fear of wolves led many to try to exterminate them from regions where settlers lived. In North America, states introduced programs to control wolves. They paid hunters a **bounty**, or reward, for killing wolves and even used poison to kill the animals. The numbers of wolves **declined** rapidly.

Wolves are **predators** that live in groups called packs. Wolf packs hunt over a large territory. A wolf pack is usually an **extended** family group that includes a male and a female, their young, and other adults.

# Species at Risk

Created in 1984, the International Union for the **Conservation** of Nature (IUCN) protects wildlife, plants, and **natural resources** around the world. Its members include about 1,400 governments and nongovernmental organizations. The IUCN publishes the Red List of Threatened **Species** each year, which tells people how likely a plant or animal species is to become **extinct**. It began publishing the list in 1964.

The western black rhinoceros of Africa was classed as Extinct (EX) by the IUCN in 2011. The IUCN updates the Red List twice a year to track the changing of species. Each individual species is reevaluated at least every five years.

## SCIENTIFIC CRITERIA

The Red List, created by scientists, divides nearly 80,000 species of plants and animals into nine categories. Criteria for each category include the growth and decline of the population size of a species. They also include how many individuals within a species can breed, or have babies. In addition, scientists include information about the **habitat** of the species, such as its size and quality. These criteria allow scientists to figure out the probability of extinction facing the species.

# IUCN LEVELS OF THREAT

The Red List uses nine categories to define the threat to a species.

| | |
|---|---|
| **Extinct (EX)** | No living individuals survive |
| **Extinct in the Wild (EW)** | Species cannot be found in its natural habitat. Exists only in **captivity**, in **cultivation**, or in an area that is not its natural habitat. |
| **Critically Endangered (CR)** | At extremely high risk of becoming extinct in the wild |
| **Endangered (EN)** | At very high risk of extinction in the wild |
| **Vulnerable (VU)** | At high risk of extinction in the wild |
| **Near Threatened (NT)** | Likely to become threatened in the near future |
| **Least Concern (LC)** | Widespread, abundant, or at low risk |
| **Data Deficient (DD)** | Not enough data to make a judgment about the species |
| **Not Evaluated (NE)** | Not yet evaluated against the criteria |

In the United States, the Endangered Species Act of 1973 was passed to protect species from possible extinction. It has its own criteria for classifying species, but they are similar to those of the IUCN. Canada introduced the Species at Risk Act in 2002. More than 530 species are protected under the act. The list of species is compiled by the Committee on the Status of Endangered Wildlife in Canada (COSEWIC).

## GRAY WOLVES AT RISK

In 1970, the IUCN established a Wolf Specialist Group. Four years later, the U.S. Fish and Wildlife Service listed the wolf as Endangered under the Endangered Species Act. In 1982, the IUCN Red List listed the gray wolf as Vulnerable. These listings helped to increase the protection of wolves in Europe and in North America. Some populations in North America have recently been **delisted**.

# Joining the Red List

Wolves are territorial animals, which means they are attached to the territory where they hunt and live. They do not often leave their territories. Where wolves' territories overlap with human settlements and farms, wolves often have been hunted to extinction. In Europe, wolves were killed or driven into **wilderness** regions because they preyed on livestock. When European settlers arrived in North America, they began farming in wolf territories. They saw the wolf as a threat to their livestock. The settlers also killed deer and elk for food. The wolf lost both its hunting territory and its food source. Without their natural prey, some wolves began to attack livestock to survive.

At first, one of the biggest challenges to protecting the gray wolf was the hostility of many people toward the animals. For example, hunters in Montana were angry that wolves were reducing the numbers of elk and other game animals in the state.

SAVE AN ELK HERD

KILL A WOLF!

Wolf packs live and hunt in territories that are between 200 to 500 square miles (515–1,300 sq. km). Because they are attached to these territories and do not often move to new areas, they are vulnerable to hunting when humans enter their territories.

# PEOPLE VS WOLVES

In the 1800s, U.S. state governments began to pay hunters to kill or trap wolves that threatened farms and livestock. Hunters set traps called snares. These loops of wire strangle wolves. Such methods of wolf control spread across the United States. In Canada, the government introduced similar methods in the 1950s. This stopped the natural **migration** of wolves into Montana and Idaho. The programs were effective. Most wolves in North America were wiped out. There are still programs to kill wolves to keep their numbers under control. However, wildlife biologists argue that there are better ways to coexist with wolves.

The U.S. Forest Service and the Bureau of Biological Survey began paying hunters to kill wolves in 1915. By 1942, more than 24,000 wolves had been killed.

# An Environment in Danger

Wolves are a **keystone species**. This means that they play a vital role in how their **ecosystem** functions. They prey on animals that, if too numerous, would overrun habitats. If a keystone species disappears or appears, there are changes all through a food chain. This, in turn, affects the ecosystem. Scientists call this trophic cascade. When wolves disappeared from their territories, the deer and elk populations grew, leading to a shortage of food for birds and other animals. Without its keystone species, the wolf, the ecosystem became unbalanced and unhealthy.

Elk and deer eat plants. When wolves disappeared from parts of North America, elk and deer populations grew larger, and the herds ate more plants. Fewer plants grew. This led to a loss of food for other species in the ecosystem, such as beavers.

# ISLE ROYALE WOLVES

The first wolves to reach Isle Royale in Lake Superior crossed an ice bridge in the late 1940s. No people live on the small island, but it is home to moose, so there is plenty of food (right). However, diseases, harsh weather, and other issues affected the wolves. By 2016, only two wolves survived. The U.S. National Park Conservation Association announced plans to introduce 20 to 30 more wolves to the island. This would help keep the moose population under control.

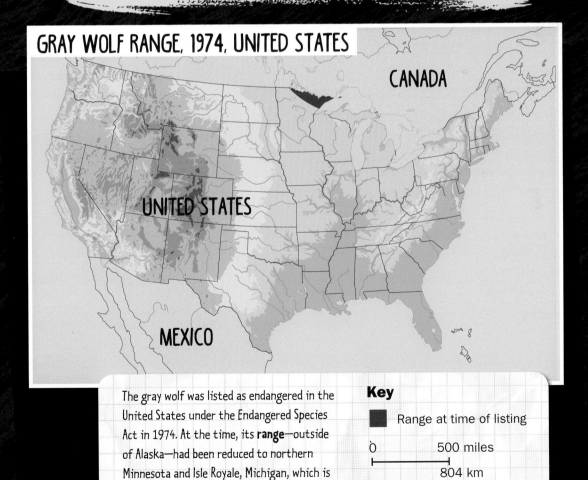

## GRAY WOLF RANGE, 1974, UNITED STATES

CANADA

UNITED STATES

MEXICO

The gray wolf was listed as endangered in the United States under the Endangered Species Act in 1974. At the time, its **range**—outside of Alaska—had been reduced to northern Minnesota and Isle Royale, Michigan, which is in Lake Superior.

**Key**

■ Range at time of listing

0          500 miles
├─────────────┤
           804 km

# Who Got Involved?

Many **conservationists**, officials, and individuals believed the wolf needed help to recover. They asked the government for action. Finally, in 1974, the U.S. Fish and Wildlife Service listed the gray wolf as Endangered under the new Endangered Species Act. Interest groups such as Defenders of Wildlife, the Wolf Fund, and the Wolf Action Group offered plans for recovery. However, not everyone believed the wolf should be saved. The American Farm Bureau Federation argued that wolves were a danger to livestock. Other groups wanted to continue hunting the wolf for its fur. Many citizens agreed.

In 1939, wildlife biologist Adolph Murie studied wolves in McKinley Park, Alaska. Today, this is Denali National Park and Preserve. He was the first to suggest that the wolf is vital to a healthy ecosystem. Murie's work changed the way people managed wildlife in parks.

Conservation plans rely on wolves breeding successfully. A female gray wolf gives birth once a year, and usually has a litter of about seven pups. For the first weeks of their lives, the pups stay with their mother, while other wolves in the pack bring them food. This helps the pups learn to mix with all members of the pack.

# COLLABORATING FOR A CAUSE

The Nez Percé of Idaho have a close bond with the gray wolf, which is an important part of their culture. In 1995, after Idaho rejected federal plans to protect wolves, the Nez Percé took responsibility for wolf recovery in the state. The Nez Percé Tribal Wildlife Program is funded by the U.S. government and is co-managed with the U.S. Fish and Wildlife Service. The Nez Percé arranged for 15 wolves to be brought from Canada that same year. Tribal **elders** welcomed them with songs. The next year, 20 more wolves arrived. The Nez Percé tracked the wolves and kept them away from livestock. If wolves did attack animals, the tribe removed them. In 2005, the State of Idaho took over wolf management. However, the Nez Percé still manage wolves on tribal lands, and run the Wolf Research and Education Center.

# An Action Plan

The U.S. Fish and Wildlife Service appointed a team to plan how to bring back the wolf. The Northern Rocky Mountain Wolf Recovery Team released its final plan in 1987. The plan focused on three recovery areas. These were places where the wolf could live and breed in safety. The areas were northwestern Montana, central Idaho, and Yellowstone National Park. The plan was to allow some wolves to migrate naturally from Canada and to release wolves in Idaho and Montana. Other wolves would be reintroduced to Yellowstone. It was difficult for everyone to agree on the plan. Many ranchers and citizens were against any wolf conservation, but scientists, wildlife organizations, and others were anxious to save the wolf. In 1991, the U.S. Congress directed the Fish and Wildlife Service to prepare an environmental impact statement (EIS) for wolf recovery. The document, outlining the plan and its impact, was finalized in 1994. It described ways in which the wolf's return would help or harm the environment.

The action plan included a program to track wolves after they had been released by fitting them with radio collars. Continuing research about the animals' movements would help scientists to adapt the plan if necessary.

# COLLABORATING FOR A CAUSE

The gray wolf has supporters across North America and around the world. There are many conservation groups in the United States, such as Defenders of Wildlife, the Wolf Fund, Earth Justice, and the Center for Biological Diversity. These groups help to educate the public about wolves, carry out research, and much more. They sometimes sue governments to make sure they protect wolves and their habitats. The International Wolf Center focuses on education. The Wolf Working Group and the IUCN **Canid** Specialist Group are international organizations. Their members are experts who create protection and management plans for wolves. They also share their research. Frequent contact with humans can be harmful to wild animals, so experts study wolves from a distance.

Wolf experts working in the wilderness in Montana use radio, binoculars, and long-distance cameras to observe a wolf pack from a safe distance.

# Making the Plan Work

The first step in the action plan was organizing the release of wolves in their new homes in the northern Rocky Mountains. Altogether, 66 wolves would be brought from Canada to the United States. Each of the three territories in Montana, Idaho, and Yellowstone needed help from wolf experts, wildlife groups, volunteers, and others. The plan relied on funding from the U.S. government and donations from the public.

Experts identified packs in Canada from which to take wolves without harming the pack. The animals were **tranquilized** and taken to their new homes by truck. Under the plan, the new arrivals were kept in large pens to settle in and get used to their new territory. When they were released into the wild, they were fitted with radio collars so they could be tracked.

Wolf sanctuaries provide a safe home for wolves that might not be able to survive in the wild. People can visit wolf sanctuaries in the United States and Canada to get a closer look at the animals and to learn more.

# COLLABORATING FOR A CAUSE

The Yellowstone National Park relocation plan relied on groups, including the IUCN World Commission on Protected Areas, the U.S. National Park Service, and Jasper National Park in Alberta, Canada. In 1995, 14 wolves from Jasper were transported to Yellowstone and released (right). By 1997, another 27 wolves had been moved to the park. The recovery plan was successful. At the end of 2016, there were 108 wolves living in Yellowstone.

## WOLVES OUTSIDE PROTECTED AREAS IN WYOMING, 2000-2017

The successful Yellowstone relocation plan has had a wider effect. Some wolves have migrated out of the national park. This graph shows the number of wolves living in Wyoming outside Yellowstone National Park and another protected area, the Wind River Reservation. While the number of wolves inside the protected areas has risen, there has also been a steady rise in the wolf population elsewhere in the state.

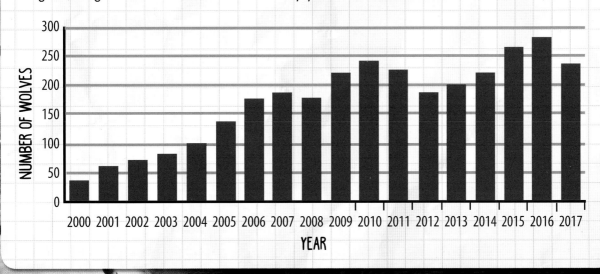

# Challenges and Solutions

Bringing back the gray wolf faced many problems. Some groups such as ranchers were never happy about the wolf's return. Providing large enough territories for the wolves was another challenge. Nevertheless, as the wolf population recovered, the U.S. Fish and Wildlife Service changed its conservation status. Between 2008 and 2010, it delisted the gray wolf twice, but federal courts reversed the decision. However, in 2011 the wolf lost its protection in Idaho, Montana, and parts of Oregon, Utah, and Washington. The wolf was delisted in Wyoming in 2012. It was relisted in 2014 and delisted again in 2017.

Wolves that live near farms still attack livestock from time to time. Farmers who lose livestock to wolves are paid for their losses by state governments or by organizations such as Defenders of Wildlife.

# COLLABORATING FOR A CAUSE

The Wood River Wolf Project began in Idaho in 2008. It brings together ranchers, conservationists, and officials, and is sponsored by Defenders of Wildlife. The project aims to find ways to protect livestock without killing wolves. One way is to use Foxlights, which look as though someone is walking around with a flashlight. Wolves are naturally wary of people, so they stay away. The project also uses electric fences lined with orange or red flags (right). The colorful flags frighten the wolves, which stay away. If they do get close, they get a warning shock. Using methods like these, the project has shown that there are ways to protect livestock without killing wolves.

# CANADIAN WOLVES

In Canada, the gray wolf is not endangered. In most parts of the country, it is a game animal, which means that people can hunt and trap wolves legally. The wolf is protected in national parks, but even inside the parks

there can be problems. For example, in Banff National Park (left), wolves have almost completely disappeared. In 2016, park rangers killed two adult wolves for going too close to campsites. Their pups died when they strayed onto a railroad. Conservationists are hoping that a new pack will form and bring the gray wolf back to the park.

# Return of the Gray Wolf

The wolf recovery plan set out the goals it hoped to achieve. After three years, it aimed to have at least 300 wolves living across the three recovery areas. In fact, it was even more successful. By 2003, the population had recovered enough for the gray wolf's status to be upgraded from Endangered to Near Threatened under the Endangered Species Act. By the end of 2011, there were about 1,774 wolves in the northern Rocky Mountains. In August 2015, California had its first wild wolf pack in almost 100 years. By 2018, there were between 5,000 to 6,000 wolves living in the lower 48 states. Even so, the gray wolf only inhabits less than 10 percent of its historical range.

Some conservationists would like to see wolves reintroduced in eastern states. However, wolf recovery in the West took many years from the first plans to the return of the wolves. Any plans to bring wolves to the East would likely take even longer to achieve.

# COLLABORATING FOR A CAUSE

In states where wolves have recovered well, such as Idaho, state officials now control wolf populations. They allow hunting seasons, for example, and watch for livestock attacks. The U.S. Fish and Wildlife Service continues to monitor wolf recovery (right). In 2014, it relisted the gray wolf in Michigan, Minnesota, and Wisconsin. The wolf also has federal protection in California and parts of Washington and Oregon.

## WOLF RECOVERY AREAS, 2018

CANADA

UNITED STATES

MEXICO

The gray wolf's range has recovered strongly from its lowest point in 1974. A combination of the deliberate release of wolves and natural migration from Canada has created new wolf packs in the Great Lakes and the northern Rocky Mountains. In the Southwest, the gray wolf's smaller cousin, the Mexican gray wolf, has been reintroduced to eastern Arizona and western New Mexico.

**Key**

■ Historical range

■ Current range

■ Southwest Recovery Area

0       500 miles

# Helping the Environment

Today, there are about 65,000 gray wolves living in the United States and Canada. Canada has the second largest population of gray wolves in the world, after Russia. In the areas where wolves have returned, the ecosystems are healthier and more balanced. **Scavengers**, such as wolverines and eagles, feed on wolf leftovers. There are fewer coyotes, because the wolves eat coyotes. Coyotes prey on smaller animals, such as gophers and beavers, and also hunt pronghorn fawns. Now these animals have a chance to live longer. Wolves often prey on weak or old animals. In this way, they help manage animal populations without stopping them growing completely.

The gray wolf's return to Yellowstone helped another animal. Like the wolf, beavers had almost disappeared from the national park. Just before wolves returned, there was only one beaver colony in the park. Today, there are nine, and the population is growing. Beavers build dams and create ponds. Fish, water birds, and other animals also began to thrive.

# HELPING PLANT LIFE

By controlling the elk and deer populations, the wolves have helped other plant-eaters, such as bison and beavers. Plant life is important. Elk like to eat aspen, cottonwood, and willow that grow along rivers. After the wolf returned, however, elk had to keep moving around to avoid wolf packs. This meant that they stopped spending as much time by rivers. As a result, Yellowstone biologists found that more plants and trees grew along the riverbeds. These plants attract more insects to the area. The insects provide food for birds, fish, and amphibians. Since the plants have time to grow without being eaten, the roots are stronger. These roots help to keep the riverbank stable, which helps to control pollution and flooding. Water quality also improves.

Conservationists argue that removing the wolf threatens the natural balance of its ecosystem with unexpected results, such as decline in water quality.

# What Does the Future Hold?

The future for the gray wolf in the lower 48 states is still uncertain. One reason is hunting. In states such as Idaho, officials now allow the hunting of wolves. They issue permits to allow hunters and trappers to kill up to five wolves each year. In states such as Indiana, wolves are still protected, but people can kill wolves that threaten them or damage property. In Yellowstone, hunting is illegal, but hunters can kill wolves that wander outside the park boundaries. A female Yellowstone wolf known as 0-Six was shot outside the park in 2012. Wolf management departments keep a close watch on the wolves in their state. Strict laws can help stop overhunting and keep the gray wolf from returning to the endangered list.

A hunter poses with a display of wolf pelts in Alaska. Wolves have never been endangered in the state, and about 1,200 are hunted every year. Hunters must still apply for permits from the state to kill wolves there.

# LIVING WITH WOLVES

The gray wolf is still endangered in areas within the United States and in Europe. In other places, it has made a strong recovery. Wild wolves may begin to migrate into some of their historical hunting grounds, as happened in parts of Washington State. In 2017, a wolf pack arrived in Denmark for the first time in more than 200 years, when it migrated from Germany. Wolves need a lot of space, however. People need to protect large regions of natural habitat for wolves and other animals and plants to survive.

Conflict continues between people who want to protect the wolf and those who see the wolf as a threat. According to the World Wildlife Fund (WWF), wolves cause less than one percent of all damage to livestock. Ranchers and farmers still fear wolf attacks on their livestock, however. There are also studies that show that killing wolves is not the answer. The WWF, Defenders of Wildlife, and other groups try to show people that wolves and livestock can live close to each other successfully. These groups promote **carcass** removal programs to bury dead livestock so the smell does not attract wolves. They encourage shepherding programs, in which ranchers stay close to their cattle to watch them. They also advise on the use of radio-activated guard systems that warn if wolves are in an area. Such methods require action from ranchers, and many ranchers remain reluctant to adopt them.

# Saving Other Species

The U.S. Fish and Wildlife Service claims that the gray wolf is no longer endangered. Many conservationists disagree. They are resisting calls to delist the gray wolf completely. They point out that delisting the wolf would be difficult because the animal's historical range has been taken over by people, towns, farms, and roads. The future of the gray wolf depends on controlling hunting and saving large areas of wilderness. Some experts believe that similar measures may help protect other species of wolf under threat in various parts of North America.

The red wolf of Florida and the southeastern United States is one of the most threatened wolves in the world. The IUCN Red List classes the animal as critically endangered, and it is listed under the Endangered Species Act.

# MEXICAN GRAY WOLF

Conservationists are concerned about the gray wolf's smaller cousin, the Mexican gray wolf. This wolf used to live in the southwestern United States and northern Mexico. It suffered from the same problems as the gray wolf in the north. Today, the Mexican gray wolf remains endangered. The U.S. Fish and Wildlife Service listed the Mexican wolf in 1976, and a recovery plan began in 1998. The Mexican wolf was reintroduced to the wild in recovery areas in eastern Arizona and western New Mexico. The recovery team released 11 Mexican gray wolves into the wild. As of 2017, the number had risen to 114 wolves.

# WOLF OF THE NORTHEAST

The Algonquin wolf is a threatened species that lives in northern Ontario and small parts of Quebec, Canada. In a 2018 report, scientists estimated that there were fewer than 1,000 Algonquin wolves. The wolf is protected in Algonquin Park, Killarney, and other parks in Ontario. However, if animals leave the parks, many are shot. A "buffer zone" around the park helps to prevent this. Wolves Ontario and other groups helped to push for the first Algonquin Wolf Recovery Strategy.

# What Can You Do to Help?

Helping the wolf is something everyone can do. Spreading awareness about the wolf and countering its negative image is vital. The more people know about the wolf and the environment, the more help the wolf will receive. Read more about the wolf's behavior and its habitat. Share what you learn at school. Your teacher may help you organize a project about the wolf and the environment. Work together with your classmates, friends, or family to think of your own action plan.

Wolf conservation organizations sometimes arrange protests to support the gray wolf. If you feel strongly about helping wolves, you can use the Internet and social media to get in touch with such organizations and discover whether they are planning any activities in your area.

It is difficult to see wolves in the wild. It is far easier to see gray wolves close up and learn about how they live at a wolf center.

# TAKE ACTION!

**Wolf Awareness Week is the third week of October. It is the perfect time to hold a local event to raise awareness of wolves. It can be at your school, a community hall, or anywhere people can gather together.**

- You can make posters and fact sheets that explain why wolves still need protection. Try creating diagrams that illustrate how the wolf is a keystone species and how it benefits the ecosystem.

- Volunteer to help a charity that works to protect the wolf, such as Livingwithwolves.org. Such organizations provide information packs to help hold local meetings, and they usually welcome offers to help raise funds for their operations.

- Write your elected representatives about why wolves are important to the ecosystem. You can also write to local newspapers to make your case. Letters can be powerful tools for change.

# Learning More

## Books

Castaldo, Nancy F. *Back from the Brink,* Houghton Mifflin Harcourt, 2018.

Gagne, Tammy. *Gray Wolf. Back from Near Extinction*. Core Library, 2017.

Jazynka, Kitson. *Mission Wolf Rescue: All About Wolves and How to Save Them.* National Geographic Kids, 2014.

McAneney, Caitie. *The Return of the Gray Wolf. Bouncing Back from Extinction*. Powerkids Press, 2017.

Saxena, Shalini. *Saving the Endangered Wolf.* Britannica Educational Publishing, 2016.

## On the Web

**www.biokids.umich.edu/critters/ Canis_lupus**
This University of Michigan site has general information about the gray wolf, aimed at younger readers.

**defenders.org/gray-wolf/ basic-facts**
Defenders of Wildlife has information on wolf conservation efforts and links to other resources.

**www.livingwithwolves.org**
This site contains details about the activities of a leading wolf conservation group, with an information brochure to download.

**www.nationalgeographic.org/ media/gray-wolf-family-activity- guide**
A downloadable guide about the gray wolf and its relatives from National Geographic.

For videos, activities, and more, enter the access code at the Crabtree Plus website below.

**www.crabtreeplus.com/animals-back-brink**

**Access code: abb37**

# Glossary

**Atlantic Canada** The region of Canada located on the Atlantic coast, comprising New Brunswick, Prince Edward Island, Nova Scotia, and Newfoundland and Labrador

**bounty** A payment for capturing or killing an animal

**canid** A member of the dog family

**captivity** The state of being kept in one place and not allowed to leave

**carcass** The body of a dead animal

**conservation** The careful management of animals, plants, and the environment

**conservationists** Experts in conservation

**critical** Very serious or dangerous

**declined** Fell in number

**delisted** Removed from the list of endangered species because the population has reached a safe number

**ecosystem** Everything that exists in a particular environment, including living things such as animals and plants and nonliving things such as the earth and sunlight, and the connections among them

**elders** Senior individuals in a tribe

**extended** Larger than usual

**exterminate** To destroy completely

**extinct** Describes a situation in which no living individuals of a species survive

**habitat** The place where an animal or plant normally lives or grows

**keystone species** An animal on which other animals and plants in a particular ecosystem depend

**livestock** Farm animals kept for use or profit

**migration** The regular movement of animals from one region to another

**natural resources** Useful materials that occur in nature

**predators** Animals that prey on, or hunt, other animals for food

**range** The geographical area in which an animal usually lives

**scavenger** A species that feeds on dead animals or plant material

**species** A group of similar animals or plants that can breed with one another

**tranquilized** Knocked out using drugs

**tundra** Areas of the world where there are no trees and the earth is frozen

**wilderness** A wild region that is uninhabited by people and not used for agriculture

# Index and About the Author

**ABOUT THE AUTHOR**

Cynthia O'Brien has written many nonfiction books for children and young adults. One of her most magical memories is hearing the wolves howl during a camping trip in Algonquin Park.